FREEDOM'S JOURNEY

Karen Garrett

Copyright © 2020
All rights reserved.

No part of this book may be reproduced or transmitted in any form or by any means, electronic or mechanical, including photocopying, recording, or by any information storage and retrieval system, without permission in writing from the copyright owner.

Published by
GRAPH Publishing, L.L.C.
www.graphpublishing.com

Printed in the U.S.A.

Table of Contents

Prologue	5
Chapter One: We Need a Plan	9
Chapter Two: Refining Fire	11
Chapter Three: The Journey Begins	15
Chapter Four: One Step at a Time	19
Chapter Five: Renewing Our Minds	23
Chapter Six: My Personal Battle	27
Chapter Seven: Learning to Lean	35
Chapter Eight: Turning Point	39
Chapter Nine: Armed for Battle	43
Chapter Ten: Baptism of the Holy Spirit	47
Chapter Eleven: Facing the Past	51
Chapter Twelve: Thoughts and Words	55
Chapter Thirteen: Transformed: Spirit vs. Flesh	59
Chapter Fourteen: Sowing the Seed	61
Chapter Fifteen: Getting to the Roots	65
Chapter Sixteen: Denying Ourselves	69
Chapter Seventeen: Paying It Forward	71
Author's Note	77

Prologue

The fact is that every one of us has been hurt-- by life's circumstances and/or by other people. And the need to be heard, to have someone to tell our stories to, can be, at times, overwhelming. In the midst of our pain we need to understand that there is Someone who always hears, always cares, and always understands, Someone who wants us to come to Him for help and forgiveness and freedom. Once we realize that there is One who cares and actually wants us to share our problems with Him and who desires to show us the way to be healed, we can come to understand the root of the hurt and why we carry the wounds, both inward and outward, that the pain has left behind.

As always, the journey to healing begins with the willingness to take the first step. We have to possess the desire, the determination, to make the changes that can bring about, not only a better way of living, but a better way of life. We need to know that it's not a quick fix; it is a process. We have to take it one step at a time…one move toward becoming wiser and whole. This process will not only help us in our journey toward healing and wellness, but will help us to understand the hurts of others as well. Eventually, we may reach a point where sharing our journey with others will help these people in theirs.

The first steps in this amazing journey begin with a sincere desire and willingness to listen, to learn, and to apply what we've learned. And, I can promise you, it won't be an easy journey. Getting to the root, or roots, of our problems and the pain that we live with usually involves opening up old wounds and facing things about ourselves and others that we'd rather not admit to, even to ourselves.

To start out, we can learn ways to make better short-term choices and reap immediate results. Just as a dieter's choosing to "pass" on eating a Snickers or a doughnut and opting for a carrot or a cup of yogurt instead, we can concentrate on making choices One positive step that we can take immediately is that we can choose to take a walk, or take up a hobby, or write a letter, or read a good book instead of poisoning our spirits by absorbing some of the trash that's available on TV.

Each seemingly minor choice that's based on wise decisions creates a forward motion that propels us toward a more positive position in life. We can reap times of refreshing instead of going around and around the same old mountain of hopelessness and despair.

It's all too easy to keep walking down the same path we've traveled before with different circumstances and different people and expect a different outcome. There's an old saying that goes like this: If we keep doing things the way we've always done them, we'll keep getting the same results we always gotten. It can be unbelievably hard to jump off that path. But there is a way to change.

The change comes when God speaks to us, and we really listen. When I finally realized that only in God could I find the courage and the wisdom to change, He began to talk to me about choices. It was not until I began to seek truth and wisdom that I was able to choose a different path.

Life as I had known it to be ceased; life as I know it can be began.

If you have come to a place in your life where you know you must do something to change the direction you've been traveling, then please join me on my journey, and we'll walk through it together.

I'm excited to be a part of your journey toward growth, healing and wisdom.

Some things I will share with you may appear very simple, but when the words I speak begin to come alive in your spirit, you may be amazed by what they can produce in your life.

I am so blessed to be able to walk with you on this journey…one of love, life, joy, encouragement, fun (yes, fun!) and freedom. As we begin, I will ask you to make a commitment, not to me, but to yourself, that you will give it your best shot. If you approach it tenuously, or without resolve, you're not likely to profit much, if any. You must commit to spending time in prayer daily, sincerely asking God to show you the roots of your problems. You'll need to trust God, even when His revelation brings up a past you'd rather not re-visit.

God is wise and loving and faithful, and as I share some of my story with you in the pages of this book, you will see that sometimes it is necessary for us to deal with memories that are painful in order to be able to recognize the truth. The Word says: "Then you shall know the truth, and the truth will set you free." (John 8:32, NIV)

But first, let's begin building our foundation. It is a basic, but powerful part of our journey. Let's start with a prayer to the One who hears and cares. Father, in Jesus' name, we thank you for the love, peace, and joy that you freely offer to each of us. Lord Jesus, we thank you for coming to earth and giving us all we needed and all you had to give. Thank you for taking the beatings that we deserved and for your obedience to the Father's will.

We thank you for the blood that flowed from your own body that washes us clean and presents us to the Father without a blemish…that you who knew no sin became sin for us that we might become the righteousness of God. (2 Corinthians 5:21)

You spoke the very words that brought us redemption and healing: "Father, forgive them, for they don't know what they're doing." (Luke 23:34, NIV) When we accept your gift of salvation and put you where you rightfully belong, on the throne of our hearts, our healing begins. You offer us the gifts of righteousness and grace, wisdom and the ability to forgive those who have wronged us. We ask, Lord Jesus, that in all our seeking, it is wisdom we strive to attain, maybe most of all.

And so, I ask that you take us by the hand and guide each person who is truly seeking this path to healing and that you open their eyes of understanding and their minds to wisdom.. Your Word tells us that "the steps of the righteous are ordered by the Lord. (Psalm 37:23, NIV)

We thank you for truth, clarity and wisdom. Jesus, we know that "If the Son sets you free, you are free indeed." (John 8:36) And that's what we're searching for…freedom from those ungodly and unhealthy things that have controlled us in the past. We thank you, and we praise you, Jesus, for your goodness and for setting the captive free…In Jesus name, Amen.

Scriptures on Which to Build Our Foundation

Romans 8:28: … and we know that all things work together for good to them that love God, to them who are the called according to His purpose. (NKJ)

John 8:36: So, if the Son sets you free, you will be free indeed. (NIV)

1 Peter 1:7: …that your faith, of greater worth than gold, which perishes even though refined by fire—may be proved genuine and may result in praise, glory and honor when Jesus Christ is revealed. (NIV)

Roman 10:11: As scripture says, everyone who believes on Him will not be put to shame. (NKJ)

Chapter One
We Need a Plan

When we start to build a new house, the very first thing we must consider is the foundation. Without a solid foundation, the house is destined to disappoint. The beams and floors and walls and the roof won't have the support they require. By the same token, when we're seeking to repair our lives, we need a firm foundation, so it can support the new life we're wanting to build in the place of the old one that didn't serve us very well.

The only sure foundation is the truth. Looking at life through rose-colored glasses, or, as more often happens, through the lens of cultural, and even demonic, influences, will cause us to flounder. Bad choices piled on top of worse choices will never prove beneficial. Neither will doing the same thing over and over again, hoping that the next time will work out better. And we absolutely must be willing to admit that at least some of the painful things that have happened to us are the direct result of poor choices on our part.

Take the example of Adam and Eve in the Garden of Eden written about in the third Chapter of Genesis. The Lord God had given them the entire garden from which to gather their food. The only exception was that they must not eat from the tree of the knowledge of good and evil. Now, to be perfectly fair, it was not Eve's fault that Satan, disguised as a serpent, came to her and tempted her to disobey God. Nor was it her fault that Satan lied to her and caused her to question God's purposes. But it absolutely was her fault that she yielded, just as Adam was responsible for his actions in following his wife's urgings.

Similarly, we are not always to blame when we are placed in difficult or sometimes brutal circumstances. But, notice what Adam said when God came calling to him in the garden after eating the forbidden fruit. He said, "That woman that YOU gave me, she gave me some of the fruit." What did he do here? First he pawned the guilt off on the woman, and then he actually blamed GOD for giving Eve to him! Adam could have chosen to obey God and refused to eat from the forbidden fruit. But he did not. There is a book named, The Silence of Adam, by Larry Crabb that deals with the repercussions of the fact that Adam remained silent instead of encouraging his wife to be obedient and tried to cast off the blame of his disobedience onto other.

So, no, we are not responsible for the actions of others, but we are definitely responsible for our own choices. Our poor or hurtful decisions will probably not have the long-lasting effects that Adam's had, but we can be assured that they will affect others adversely.

Chapter Two
Refining Fire

And I will bring the third part through the fire, and will refine them as silver is refined, and will try them as gold is tried: they shall call on my Name, and I will hear them: I will say, it is My people: and they shall say, the Lord is My God.
Zechariah 13:9 (NKJ)

Here is an illustration that I'd like to share with you that will perhaps paint a word picture to help you get a grasp of the idea behind this new journey. Hopefully, it will help you understand what God wants to do to help you. It begins with a story of a goldsmith and how he purifies the gold. Remember the verse in the first chapter that talks about how our faith is of greater worth, both to us and to our Maker, than even the purist gold.

To refine the gold, the goldsmith takes the raw gold and puts it into a vat or kettle. He builds a fire under it that will be hot enough to melt the gold. As the gold melts, the impurities in it rise to the top. He skims the impurities, called "dross", off the top. Once they have been removed, he makes the fire even hotter. He repeats this step as many times as necessary, skimming off the dross with each additional heating until nothing is left but the pure gold. You might ask how the goldsmith knows when all the impurities have been removed. The answer is: when he can see his reflection in the gold.

Think about it. God wants to refine us until He, and the world, can see His reflection in us. Cool, huh?

What I hope you'll understand is that when we embark on this journey with God, He will likely take us places where we really don't want to go. He is, in essence, the goldsmith, and we, and our faith, are the gold He is refining. We will experience the heat of the refiner's fire, and it will hurt. We will wonder what God is doing. We might reason that if we're trying to follow Him, why are we hurting? That's a very valid question and one that everyone I know asks.

One thing we need to consider is what Jesus says in John 15:16: "You did not choose me, but I chose you, and appointed you to go and bear fruit—fruit that will last…" We're chosen! That means that we are valuable to God. But, just as the impurities have to be removed from the gold, the "junk" has to be removed from our lives and our spirits before we can produce fruit for the Kingdom. I hope this little book will serve as a guide, but please remember that God is the Healer. He chose us, but, ultimately, we have to choose Him, too.

Sometimes, when a wound has "healed over," but is still festering beneath the scab, a surgeon will have to open it up again to remove the infection. And that hurts! God often does the same things with our wounds. He will be bringing them to the surface of your heart and spirit to help you take a look at them. He wants us to see and understand that the schemes Satan has used to hurt us does not define who we are.

It is as this point that we have a choice to make. We can invite God in to remove the impurities, or we can hold on to them, preferring the familiar over the promise of something much better. God never forces us to let go. He encourages, but the choice is ours. I can tell you that there will be moments when you will not understand what you're going through, when the refiner's fire burns too hot. It is in these times when our faith is tested. What may look and feel like punishment is actually an act of love. If we will wait and trust Him, He will help us see. Until then, we need to walk by faith in His heart and in His character and not by what we see or feel.

For we walk by faith not by sight. (NKJ) 2 Corinthians 5:7

Below are some Scriptures to help and encourage us on our journey to healing.

> "For I know the plans I have for you," declares the Lord, "plans to prosper you and not to harm you, plans to give you a hope and a future." Jeremiah 29:11

> Praise be to the God and Father of our Lord Jesus Christ, who has blessed us in the heavenly realms with every spiritual blessing in Christ. For He chose us in Him before the foundation of the worl to be holy and blameless in His sight. Ephesians 1:3-4 (NIV)

> Do not be conformed to the pattern of this world, but be transformed by the renewing of your mind. Then you will be able o test and approve what God's will is- His good, pleasing and perfect will. Romans 12:2 (NIV)

> Luke 4: 18 The Spirit of the Lord is upon Me, because He has anointed Me to preach the good news to the poor. He has sent me to heal the brokenhearted, to preach freedom to the captives, and recovering of sight to the blind, to release the oppressed…. (NIV)

Chapter Three
The Journey Begins

I started on my own personal journey toward spiritual and physical wellness in 1994. The world as I knew it was completely skewed. I was so messed up, and my heart was broken into so many pieces, that I doubted that anyone, even Jesus, could set it to rights again. The old saying is that you can't see the need to climb up out of the "pit" until you hit rock bottom. That was my case. I had reached the point where the choice was, literally, life or death.

The early years of my life did not revolve around church or a relationship with the Father who made me, who made all of us. My parents were believers while we did not attend church, but I had grandmother who attended church and knew how to pray. After my parents separated, my brother and I went to live with our grandmother and grandfather. Their love for each other and for us was demonstrated on a daily basis. They were kind to us; they loved and protected us in every way they knew how. They fought for custody of us when my parents were going through a divorce. Although I was very young at the time, the loving home environment made a deep impression on my heart and mind. We knew we were loved, and that we were safe. I've always felt that my grandmother never stopped praying for us.

Unfortunately, when my parents decided to remarry, I was taken from my grandparents and moved back with my mother and father. Since I was only four years old, I was aware that my world was changing, but didn't understand why nor what was happening.

From the outside looking in, my life seemed normal. In many respects, my dad was a good man. He was willing to help people in need and was held in high regard by those in the community. My mom was fun-loving and full of laughter and enjoyed coming up with ideas that led to wonderful adventures.

But there was a dark side, a not-so-pleasant side, to our home life. It was not what I wanted, nor needed, it to be. The villain in this setting was alcohol. My dad liked to drink, and when he did, he became loud and abusive. My brother and I soon learned to make ourselves scarce during these times. As I grew older, my father sought out my company more and more. For the most part, he just wanted someone to listen while he talked on, and on, and on. I was compelled to sit and listen. Mostly, I complied, but occasionally I got to the point that I had had enough and sassed him.

Apparently, my presence filled an unconscious need in him. But he wasn't concerned with meeting my needs. I always wanted my dad to teach me what he knew, like how to repair things that were broken. When given the opportunity, I would watch him at his work. On the days that he stayed away from alcohol, I enjoyed being with him. He had considerable knowledge about a lot of different subjects, and he could be very funny when he wanted to be.

But there was a place inside my heart that was empty and could only be filled by the love of a father. I think that in our society, some dads feel like they are disposable…that their only function is to bring home a paycheck and keep household things working. They often don't realize the vital role that has been handed to them. Sons and daughters, both, need the love, acceptance and affirmation from their paternal parent, as well as from their mothers.

Mostly, I just wanted my dad to love me as a father loves his daughters. My dad either didn't recognize this need and his responsibility to fill it, or he didn't know how to fill those needs of a daughter. I believe this lack of affirmation and self-worth set me on the path of looking for acceptance like my grandparents had given me. The flip side was that I didn't have any idea of what that looked like. I didn't know what qualities to look for, so I made some wrong choices. I had seen no example of how to build a healthy relationship, so instead of working on the one I was in at the time, I would chunk that one and moved on into another one. For many years, my life followed this pattern.

I wanted a safe place for my family, but my choices did not reflect that desire. I was caught in a vicious cycle. The way I chose each time I started over guaranteed that the path I was walking would always end up looking more and more like the life I had just left. That's not what I wanted, and I hated the vicious cycle I was in. I always felt challenged to show the men I loved that our life together could be good. My attitude was one that said, "Just let me love you and show you how it can be better."

Let me tell you right now, that doesn't work. As good as it might sound, we can't love people into changing. I was not created to be the one who could bring it all together, to bring life into proper focus. In all my relationships with men, I was searching for someone who would love me and protect me. I was looking for the love and approval that I had never received from my dad. But at the end of each search lay yet another disappointment. Each time my heart was shattered, I just picked myself up and decided to try again, this time assuring myself that I wasn't going to allow anyone to hurt me again.

By the time my journey with Jesus began, I was broken and lost. I had made so many poor choices that I wasn't sure I could ever recover, much less move on. I wanted to "get it right" the next time. I was so broken and full of fear that when one of my children would ask a simple question like, "What's for supper?," I would panic. My reaction was, "NO! Not another decision. What if I make the wrong one?"

In reality, a benign question like that would not provoke any type of extreme reaction. A normal person would know it was just a meal, decide what to serve, and just cook it. But I felt like a virtual avalanche of wrong decisions and choices was falling over me, and I couldn't see the road signs. Memories of wrong turns and dead ends had pretty much paralyzed my decision-making abilities. This time I wasn't able to "pick myself up, dust myself off, and start all over again."

I didn't really even know who I was any more, because I had tried so hard to be what each man in my life had wanted me to be, I lost a sense of my own identity. I felt like I was drowning in a roiling, turbid sea, uncertain that I could find my way out.

The problem was that I didn't have a firm foundation to build on. All I had were ideas of how life and love could be and should be, and I wanted that life more than anything.

What I've learned through all those poor choices and broken dreams is that no man could give me what I had been searching for.

And so, my journey began. I don't know where you are in your life's walk, but I do know that, whatever the question is, God is the answer. He is our safe place. We will find our truth in His love and wisdom. His Word says that we will know the truth, and the truth will set us free.

You might ask, "Free from what?" One thing we are free from when we know the truth, and this is a "biggie," is condemnation. Our own personal truths do not condemn us. Once we accept the Truth about who Jesus is and what He has done for us, we are free from condemnation. In Romans 8:1 the Word also says that there is now no condemnation for those who are in Christ Jesus. The world may condemn us; we may condemn ourselves, but in God's eyes, once we have acknowledged what Jesus did on the cross and made Him Lord of our lives, we have been washed in the blood of the Lamb and are now, therefore, spotless.

What you will discover as you seek Him is that the truth does not condemn you. We seek that Truth when we are tired of all the other "solutions" and self-improvement rhetoric that have left us no better off than we were before. God's Truth will change us from the inside, out.

I am no longer the person that I once was. When we become believers, the Holy Spirit comes to live in us, and we become new creatures. I stopped trying to fix my mistakes or explain to my children why I made the choices I made. My heart hurts for them and all they endured and how those things affected them. But I cannot go back and change what happened. But God did, in fact, heal my broken heart and has shown me the way to live, to love, and to enjoy life. That doesn't mean that every choice I make now is the best one. Old habits die hard.

Chapter Four
One Step at a Time

The truth is, we walk one step at a time, and the best we can do when we fail is to accept it, admit it, repent, and get up and try to do better the next time. The purpose of this book is to guide and show us how by seeking God and His ways and plans for us sets us free. And each truth we come face-to-face with will accomplish what God plans for it to do.

As we walk one step at a time, the best we can ask of ourselves is to not try to justify wrong choices or poor behavior. We must realize that just because someone said something we did not agree with or like, we do not have the right to act out or judge him or her. This book is designed to guide and teach us how to see change inside of us. It is designed to show you that, by seeking God and His ways and plans for us, that each step to seeking the truth that sets us free will do just what God intended it to do.

But reading this little book won't accomplish anything unless you are willing to make a commitment to join in this search with a heart willing to take each step by faith. I can assure you that there will be times when you are getting to the root of a problem you've dealt with, that the hurt will seem greater than you can bear, and you will want to stop. I urge you to hang on, to understand that there is something waiting for you on the other side of your pain. Once you have sought Jesus to reveal the purpose to face the truth of your pain and to heal the wound. The choice is reject it or claim the freedom that God has offered you. These are times when all you can say is, "Lord, I trust you. I don't understand what you are doing here, but I trust you."

I want to encourage you to find, if you can, one friend you can trust who will pray with you and for you during this journey. If you don't have someone like that in your life, you might explore sites like "ministries on-line" where you can enter your prayer request. You may also feel the need to talk to someone about what you are going through. I urge you to begin keeping a journal where you can write about what you're experiencing. Be sure to date your entries so you can look back at a later date and realize what God has done and how He has helped you.

It is seldom a good idea to try to explain to those who have wounded you or those whom have hurt that you are trying to forgive them. This is usually counterproductive, and can lead to more unpleasant experiences. There may come a time when God will open the door for you to confront them, but now is not it. Wait on God's timing to share with others what you have experienced.

In James 1:5, we learn that if we ask for wisdom, God will give it generously without finding fault: "If any of you lacks wisdom, he should ask God, who gives generously to all without finding fault, and it will be given to him." This is a precious promise. God wants us to seek to be wise, so He grants wisdom without passing judgment. Wisdom in our journey is of utmost importance. When I tried to explain to my daughters why I made the choices I had made, I did so, hoping it would help them understand that I never meant to hurt them. However, the look in their eyes convinced me that I was not helping at all. Instead, my explanations seemed to cause them more pain. God explained to me that I didn't know what was in their hearts, and Satan was taking my words and using them as a knife, and driving it deeper and deeper into their hearts. We can't see what is in the hearts of others, nor how Satan can take our words and use those words to hurt them. They often cannot hear ours words, because the thoughts we are trying to express are being filtered through deep-seated wounds. God said that only He could heal them. So, now I trust God to do just that. Now, you and I can agree together to pray for those we've hurt and to aid in their healing by speaking His Word to our loved ones. Scripture says that "the Word of God is living and active and sharper than any two-edged sword." (Hebrews 4:12)

Paul, in his letter to the Romans (4:17) quotes Genesis (17:5) where God calls Abraham the father of many, even though Abraham at the time had no children at all. He refers to "God, who quickens (brings to life) the dead and calls those things which are not, as though they were." We need to speak God's Words over our loved ones, claiming His promises to heal, to make whole, with nothing missing and nothing broken. This is our best approach until God allows us to share.

Don't be a weapon Satan can use against others. I never intended to hurt my girls nor see how much I could mess up their lives. We need to understand the spirit of temptation. We will be tempted to try to explain and feel the need to justify our actions and feelings. But we are to seek the guidance of the Holy Spirit and ask Him to give us wisdom that comes from God, not from our own emotions.

These are some building blocks we'll need to lay in our foundation. Remember that our focus is on being healed. We'll need to pray for a different mind-set, for the wisdom and the way to change habits that have become ingrained over many years. We walk by faith one step at a time, and the more we understand, the easier will be the walk

Chapter Five
Renewing Our Minds

Let's talk about some ways we can begin to renew our minds for this journey toward freedom and healing.

One of the most potent verses I've found is one that God showed me and that I still refer to today. It often gives me the strength and wisdom I need to move forward, to guide me and help me focus my attention on the purpose of this journey. It can help you, too. I hope you'll memorize it.

In Luke 6: 37 we find the words, "Do not judge, and you shall not be judged; do not condemn, and you will not be condemned. Forgive, and you will be forgiven." It's so easy to look at something others have done and condemn them for it. But when we take a close look at ourselves, we can find the same kinds of thoughts and actions we see in them. Let God be the judge, and if vengeance needs to be taken, He will do it. We need to be able to forgive, for our own sakes even more than for the sakes of others. To allow a spirit of resentment or hurt or anger or revenge to fester in our spirits moves us out of the realm of the forgiven. In order to move on, we have to shut the door on parts of our past lives.

Another enemy we need to conquer is fear. At least eighty times the Scriptures tell us not to fear. Fear is an extremely effective tool the devil uses to control us, in effect, to paralyze us and keep us from moving into the realm where peace and freedom reign.

In Isaiah Chapter 43, verse 1, God says, "Do not fear, for I have redeemed you; I have called you by name; you are mine." Did you hear that? He calls us by our names! He knows us completely, and He's got this.

Other powerful verses concerning fear include:

> 2 Timothy 1:7 For God did not give us the spirit of fear, but of power and love and a sound mind.

> Joshua 1:9 Have I not commanded you? Be strong and courageous. Do not be terrified; do not be discouraged, for the Lord your God will be with you wherever you go.

> Psalm 27:1 The Lord is my light and my salvation—whom shall I fear?

"Fear not for I am with you." These are the words that God spoke to me repeatedly. I spoke these words to myself over and over again. During your journey Satan will use fear to try to grab hold of you and keep you from moving forward. When confronting our hurts, fear will try to keep you from remembering and conquering. It will say, "You lived through it once, why should you need to relive it?" If God brings you to a painful moment in your life, His purpose is not to bring you additional pain, but to heal you. God's way is to reveal the truth because it is only by knowing the truth that we will be set free. No, God doesn't want to hurt you repeatedly, not a bit of it. But Satan, the enemy, does. God will take you to places in your past to reveal the truth and to uncover the roots of your hurt and rejection. Satan wants us to fear going down this path so we will be kept in bondage to it. Fear is a prison cell in which we are constantly reminded that we are powerless—that we must suffer forever because of what we've done or what others have done to us. But, with God's help we can claim authority over fear and bind it. Then we can destroy fear at its roots so that it cannot produce a crop of anxiety and dread and failure.

To help us in conquering fear we must begin to say, "I will not be afraid." When we feel afraid to take the next step on this journey, we can be sure that the fear we are experiencing is coming from the enemy. The word of God clearly tells us that God has not given us a spirit of fear but of love, power, and a sound mind. Remember…one step at a time. This book is not written so that you can read it through and get it all done at once. We are to take it one step at a time, at the pace set by God. So, please do not be in a rush, because the Word tells us, "The steps of a good man are established by the LORD…" Psalm 37:23 (RSV)

Phil. 4:6 directs us, "Do not be anxious about anything, but in e erything by prayer and supplication, with thanksgiving, let your request be made known to God.

The purpose of the refining fire of God is to bring to the surface the impurities so that we can take a look at them. Doing so gives us the choice of keeping the impurities we see, or allowing God to remove them. God will not force the freedom He offers on any of us. He is a gentleman; he doesn't push against our wills. In fact, God knows that the reason many of His people will perish is from the lack of knowledge. But He also tells us that love rejoices in the truth. (1 Corinthians 13:6, NIV)

Taking one step at a time can also be compared to peeling back an onion one layer of skin at a time. So, I have set before you some real truths about this journey. I have shown you that you will need to be willing to see the truth from God's point of view. I can also assure you that once you are able see things as God sees them, you will know love in ways you never understood or thought possible. You can know how deep and wide and real His love is. You may at times even know the delight of feeling his arms wrapped around you, holding you and comforting you. Bottom line…God is real, and His love heals.

Chapter Six
My Personal Battle

As I mentioned before, my journey toward healing began in December of 1994. I remember looking out my dining room window and making this statement, "God, if this is all my life is, and all it will be, then, I don't mean to be rude, but I don't want it anymore."

As I stood there, I heard this small voice reply, "But what if it's not?"

I answered in desperation, "Then show me my purpose."

God's next response to me was a simple question, but it brought things into focus. He asked me to remember the last time I was truly happy. As I stood there next to the counter, the answer came to me. I saw my life being played out like a movie in front of me and realized that the only time I had ever been happy was during the interval that I spent in my grandparents' home when I was three years old. I could still feel the safety in that home and the love that had flowed freely between them and from them.

My heart just broke then, and all I could think was how sad it was that the only time I remember being happy was when I had been three years old. This realization floored me, literally, as my knees buckled, and I fell to the floor, weeping from the depths of my heart.

My journey was just beginning, and I wasn't sure where to anchor my hope. The only thing I knew for sure was that I had to trust Jesus. I needed the truth, and I knew that Jesus wouldn't lie to me. Are you ready to discover your truth?

Nothing but the truth would do. If I wasn't going to be told the truth, then the world and those in it could keep their lies and leave me alone. I had reached the point that I hated lies and was not going to accept them as a part of my life anymore. The point on which I stood was the point of life or death. Satan was trying to convince me to commit suicide by reminding me of all the wrong choices I had made. I had even gone so far as to plan how I would end my own life. He was whispering in my ear that by killing myself, I would hurt my family one last time, and then I couldn't hurt them anymore.

Many people come to this conclusion at some point in their lives. If you have considered suicide, let me assure you of one vital truth. The only thing death finalizes is our lives on earth. There is the matter of eternity. Leaving this natural world does not eradicate the fact that we will spend eternity somewhere and with someone. The devil may try to convince you that you and everyone your life has touched will be better if you are dead.
I understand this way of thinking; I've walked down that road myself. But we're seeking the truth here, aren't we? And that is not the truth. My dad's suicide ended his earthly existence, but left me with a lot of pain and many unanswered questions.

You may ask why…why did I decide to turn to Jesus instead of taking the easy way out? The answer is simple: I love my daughters and my family. I didn't want to hurt them anymore. And I hoped to be able to make it up to them for the way I had treated them before. I wanted a fresh start, and that's what Jesus promises.

So, I invited Jesus into my heart. His presence enabled me to handle the pains of withdrawal from an addiction to cocaine. And the experience was severe. Each night my whole body, from the top of my head to the soles of my feet, would shake and spasm. I spent many nights sitting in the middle of my bed with my arms wrapped around my knees, shaking and hearing the voices of the demons telling me to just go ahead and get a fix to stop the shaking.

Some of you may have experienced the same thing. It's hard to understand the severity of the hold an addictive substance can exert on its victims. When you try to fight it, there are demons who will try to control your thoughts and will continue their assault until you submit to their demands. Those demons need to be given the substance that they feed on!

Night time was the hardest time of the day for me because it was in the evening that I and the man who was my husband at the time would start "using." My fight to be free would have been futile without the help of Jesus. I would pray, "Lord, please do not let my feet hit the floor because if they do, I'm heading out the door to get my "fix." At those times I would feel his arms wrap around me and comfort me. When the withdrawal pains and spasms would stop, I would be mentally and physically exhausted and fall asleep. It was a real and constant battle, and without Jesus I could not have made it. And then I wouldn't even be here to tell my story.

Addictions can come in many forms. People can be addicted to drugs, sex, food, unhealthy relationships, self-abuse, the need for attention, pessimism, and many others. Addictions are easy to walk into, not easy at all to walk away from. Almost nobody enters into any kind of addiction on purpose. But what starts out as a seemingly harmless and temporary pleasure can quickly turn into an ugly monster, controlling our thoughts, actions, and way of life.

Scripture tell us that "There is a way that seems right to man, but leads in the end to death." (Romans 14:12) The death that the Word is talking about here is not only physical death, but eternal separation from God.

The journey we are embarked upon asks us to reject the wounds of the past. We need to learn to live without the rejection and addiction and anger that fuel our days. We need to learn to let go of the past, and that includes not hanging on to the anger and resentment we feel towards the people whom Satan has used to hurt us. The only way we can possibly do that is to learn how to forgive. And this isn't easy. But the Bible tells us that we can only be forgiven ourselves if we learn how to offer it to others. God will probably ask us to distance ourselves from some relationships and people, but the change will be a good one and has so much more to offer than a life full of drama. Begin to pray and ask God to prepare your heart for the new life of freedom.

Being creatures of habit, we all have a "comfort zone." It may not be all that "comfortable," but it's what we're familiar with. In our "familiar" zone, drama may be a normal and expected part of our days. Even in the midst of all the unhealthy things that go on, we know how to make it through the highs and lows. However we may not get through them all that well, which is why we need to pray for wisdom and the willingness to change. Even a prison cell can become familiar, and the thought of moving away from it can be stressful.

If there is a lot of drama in our lives, we can experience many conflicting emotions; one minute we may be happy, and the next moment we are upset—yelling, screaming, crying, ready to just give up and quit. We may have talked until we are blue in the face and told those who are causing such distress that we are "done." This pattern of highs and lows, of happiness and extreme anger is often repeated daily. We can become accustomed to this way of life, but it is not the way we were created to live. It is not God's plan for us to be filled with hurt and rejection, anger and rage. Nor did He create us to tolerate demonic influences in our lives. The Word of God tells us in Ephesians 6:10-13 to "be strong in the Lord and in His mighty power." We are directed to "put on the full armor of God" so that we "may be able to stand" against the wiles of the devil.

It's hard to see it sometimes, but our enemies are not people. "For we wrestle not against flesh and blood, but against the principalities, against the powers, against the rulers of this dark world, against spiritual wickedness in high places. Therefore we are to "take on the whole armor of God, so that when the day of evil comes, we may be able to stand our ground and after we have done everything, to stand." (Ephesians 6:12) That is, after all, our goal—after the battle is over to be still standing!

There is a problem, though. Many of us don't know how to do that. We need to ask Jesus to show us, to prepare us and teach us how to live in His truth and in the freedom that only He can give us. By His example we can learn how to be calm in the midst of the storm, knowing that He will see us safely through to the other side.

When we, through the strength of Jesus, have mastered the storm and come out on the other side, we'll have an amazing story to tell. Please allow me to share mine with you. There is a song called, "The Alabaster Box," which claims that no one can know the cost of the oil in a person's box. You weren't there the night Jesus came to me where I was and I found Him. I don't know the cost of the oil in your box, either. I don't know where you were when Jesus found you. But I'm so thankful that we are both making the choice to find out what His purpose for us is. What amazing love our God revealed when He allowed His only Son to take our place on the Cross of Calvary! When we can accept the fact of His undying love, we can begin to trust Him with our minds and our hearts.

One of the most precious books in the Bible is the book of John. I encourage you, in your search to find God, that you read this whole book, from beginning to end.

Here are some Scriptures that we need to memorize so we can call on them when we are uncertain.

> For God so loved the world that he gave his only begotten Son, that whosoever believes in him should not perish, but have everlasting life. John 3:16
>
> (v.17) For God did not send his Son into the world to condemn the world, but that the world, through him, might be saved.
>
> (v.18) He that believes on him is not condemned: but he that doesn't believe is condemned already, because he has not believed in the name of the only begotten Son of God.
>
> (v.19) And this is the condemnation, that light is come into the world, and men loved darkness rather than light, because their deeds were evil.
>
> (v.20) For everyone that does evil hates the light, nor does he come to the light, for fear that his deeds will be exposed.
>
> (v.21) But whoever lives by the truth comes into the light, so it may be seen plainly that what he has done has been done through God.

There is no higher form of truth than what God has said. God sent His only begotten Son to earth so that in His life He would fulfill the law given in the Old Testament, and that His death on the cross would pay, in full, the debt we owe to God for our disobedience. The Ten Commandments found in the book of Exodus in the Old Testament were given to reveal to us God's demand for perfection and to show us that, in and of ourselves, we are powerless to keep them.

They are our standard, but they are also our accusers, pointing the way to the need for a Redeemer. The Ten Commandments were written to reveal the weakness of the flesh and prove to us that people cannot live in the flesh, leaning upon our own understanding and abilities to fulfill the law. Proverbs 3:5-6 says we are to trust in the Lord with all your heart and lean not upon your own understanding. In all your ways acknowledge (or submit) to him, and He will make your path straight." (NIV)

By watching my grandmother live her life trusting God, I learned that Jesus would always tell me the truth. I also understood that each of us has a "God-sized" hole in our hearts that only He can fill. I know, and if you're like me, you know that, too. I had searched everywhere trying to find something that would fill that void, only to end up feeling empty. None of the relationships I had been in had been completely satisfying, either.

That is why, on that December day back in 1994, I was searching for something, although I was not quite sure what it was. I did have this belief that when I found it, I would know it. That day I was looking for the truth, and I found it. His name is Jesus, the Christ. Since that time, my life has never been the same. The journey God took me on was not easy; the search for truth seldom is.

Today, I can look back over my journey and recognize every place that Jesus carried me, everywhere His love and strength made me strong where, previously, I had been weak. I truly don't know how I survived so long without Him.

The night came when I wanted to stop using cocaine. The man I was married to at the time had gone to buy some for us to use. I was sitting at the end of our bed. Opposite the bed was a dresser with a mirror. I remember sitting there crying out to Jesus.

"Lord," I said, "please, help me! I want to stop!" At that moment my husband came back home and into the bedroom. My girls were asleep in their rooms with their doors closed. I just sat there and watched while he rigged up the cocaine. When he told me to give him my arm, I said, "I don't want to do this anymore. Let's stop." I turned to him and looked him square in the eyes and said, "Let's stop. I love you, and I want us to have a better life than this. You said you wanted to stop, too. Please."

At that time I didn't know about the demons of addiction and how they can control a person. My husband just looked at me and said, "Yeah, sure.

Now give me your arm." Finally, I offered my arm and said, "OK, then, give me enough to kill me."

He shot me up, not realizing how pure the cocaine was. A short while after it hit my system, I couldn't even speak. The sounds that came out of my mouth were just noise. He had already shot himself up and was out of the room. I fell to the floor, lying on my back and staring at the ceiling. I knew I was dying, but didn't even care. My body had already become numb, and I was powerless to even move, much less get up off the floor. My eyes were focused on the ceiling, and I was aware that I had quit breathing.

Then I heard someone telling me to breathe; the words reached my mind, and I took another breath. Lying there staring at the ceiling, I was numb and void of all emotions. Then someone spoke again, once more telling me to breathe. I'm not sure how long this went on because I lost all track of time. Eventually I was able to move again, so I crawled into the shower and turned on the cold water. This would cause my blood vessels to contract and slow the progression of the cocaine in my body.

Once the effects of the drug began to wear off, I went to my husband, who was in the living room, and asked for another shot. Finally, he was able to rig up another one, and he shot me up again.

Did you ever see the movie, "Ghost" with Patrick Swayze. There was a scene in which there were black shadows that came up from the ground to get the person who was dead or dying and take them on to hell. Those shadows were very real to me that night. I saw them coming up out of the floor to get me. I kept telling them to go away and leave me alone.

That night was the last time I used drugs. When I came down from the "high" the next morning, I was so upset with myself for giving in to the voices of the demons. That same day, my husband's girlfriend came to my job. When I got home, I packed up his things and moved him out and moved on with my life, a different life, one founded on the truth of Jesus Christ.

I realized that I had come to the end of "me", and that I didn't have the wisdom or strength to change. I needed help; I needed Jesus. I had tried to stop using many times before but always regressed.

In this journey we will come to places that bring us to the very end of our own ability to make changes in our life situations. And while the journey is great and fulfilling, it can also demand that we humble ourselves and learn to trust Him in every area of our lives.

Chapter Seven
Learning to Lean

Fear not, for I am with you.
Be not dismayed, for I am your God.
I will strengthen you. Yes, I will help you;
I will uphold you with my righteous right hand. Isaiah 41:10 (NKJV)

Coming to the end of ourselves simply means that we realize how impotent we are. All our knowledge and talent is God-given. On our own, we have nothing. We begin to understand that God's thoughts and ways are higher than our own. Matthew 7:7(NKJ) Ask, and it will be given to you; seek and you will find; knock, and it will be opened to you.

What we do need to do is work on building a relationship with the One who loves us and knows us best. When we try to take the reins and chart our own course, we will inevitably mess up. The promise is that when we acknowledge Him in all our thoughts and plans, He will make the path straight.

One of the main goals of our journey is to come to recognize the places inside our hearts that need healing. We will become aware of them as we begin to renew our minds by reading and absorbing the Word of God. The world offers many attitudes that are contrary to the ideal and the truth. We may even unconsciously say things that imply the opposite meaning.

For example, back in the 70's we might have said, "That's bad," when we were really meaning, "that's good." Sometimes we may or may not be sure of what people are really meaning when they comment about other people or subjects. They may be speaking candidly, or there might be sarcasm or an underlying message behind their words. Using casual slang or idioms is not necessarily wrong, but as we walk this path we've chosen, we come to realize the power of our words. This recognition should encourage us to think before we speak. In Proverbs 18:21 we hear, "The tongue has the power of life and death, and those who love it will eat its fruit." (NIV)

Let's think about that for a minute. If we say something like, "I'd like to wring his neck," or "I could just die," are we speaking life or death? Yes, those are just ways of voicing frustration or discouragement, but do we want to eat the fruits of our words? When we speak, our words carry with them life or death. Sure, we may have said something like that a hundred times, and you and the person you're angry with are still alive. But what door did we open? If the people we were upset with actually did die, how would we feel? Relieved? Guilty? God is the author and giver of life. Sin and Satan offer death. We will delve into that more deeply as we pursue the course we've embarked on. For now, I really want us to begin to renew our minds. One of the first steps we need to take is to consciously notice and begin to change our speech patterns. Remember that the words we speak offer to ourselves and others either life, or death.

Now, the question we have to ask ourselves is, do we truly desire to know the truth? Finding the answer is the key to realizing what we hold important in our life journey. Some would rather not know, and others might even fear the truth. Remember our verse from 2 Timothy? God does not give us the spirit of fear. Satan does. He can control us when he controls what we fear. Sometimes false impressions seem to be true. We can hang on to those because they are familiar, or we can go out on the limb of trust and delve into the mysteries that bring knowledge of what is genuinely true. Oswald Chambers says, "Out on a limb with God is the safest place you can be."(fom My Utmost for His highest)

The next probing question we need to ask is, "Why would anyone be afraid to know the truth?" The deepest and most reliable truth is found in the Word of God. In 1 John 4:18, we read, "There is no fear in love. But perfect love drives out fear, because fear has to do with tornment. The one who fears is not made perfect in love."

The purpose of this chapter is to establish a foundation, based on the truth, that will help us in our journey. We need to understand that, in facing our past, we will come across things that provoke the fear that we're seeking to avoid. We need to learn to face our fears with God's help. Every time we face our fears, God will reveal the truth, and some of the wounds we've received will begin to heal.

Our goal is to deal with every part of our lives that Satan has hurt, every time he hurt and deceived us. The temptation is to relate the pain to the people who caused the pain. And there is a measure of authenticity to that idea. People do hurt us, deceive and use us. We may have experienced abuse in many different forms, and no one deserves to be abused. But when we can reconcile ourselves with the fact that Satan was the one pulling the strings, we can begin to understand what Jesus knew better than anyone. No one more innocent than He ever suffered more undeserved abuse. But when He was hanging on that cross, the cross that we deserved, His words were, "Father, forgive them because they don't know what they are doing." (Luke 23:34, NIV)

He knew that the ones who were crucifying Him were unconsciously allowing themselves to be Satan's minions, to carry out Satan's plans. And so, He understanding to power of the Father to forgiveness. How could He do that? He knew them by name and could have called down ten thousand angels to come and rescue Him from the cross and bring down curses on those who were torturing and mocking Him. But He didn't. And His willingness to forgive should inspire and encourage us to begin to forgive those who have hurt us.

Jesus had a choice. He could have looked at all the sin in the world, and the people who were rejecting Him, turned His back and walked away. But He knew He was their, and our, only hope for redemption and an eternity in Heaven. 2 Corinthians 5:21 says, "God made him who had no sin to be sin for us, so that in Him we might become the righteousness of God." (NIV)

He took all the sins of the world, and even our sin natures, on Himself, so that we might become His righteousness. In so doing He offered to us the gift of grace and forgiveness. The words of the Lord's Prayer come to both encourage and convict us. "Forgive us our sins, as we forgive those who sin against us." We can be forgiven only to the extent that we offer forgiveness to others.

It helps to remember that our battle is not against flesh and blood. Our foe is much more powerful than mortal man. As we continue this journey, we build it on the foundation of truth. When we sincerely desire to know the truth, we will arrive at the place where God is taking us with the goal of healing. He will open our eyes of truth and understanding.

Chapter Eight
Turning Point

I came to this place in the beginning of my journey. I must say that in those beginning days I was given a life line to hold on to, and hold on I did. However, what I wasn't aware of is that I was full of fear. If anyone had asked me what it was that frightened me, I would have looked him or her straight in the eye with a glare of defiance in my own and said, "Nothing. I'm not afraid of anyone or anything." I believed that that was true. I viewed any show of fear as a sign of weakness, and in the world I was living in, it wasn't safe to let anyone know you were afraid.

When I did occasionally slip and let the fear inside of me show, my boyfriend would smile. He knew he had the upper hand, so he would hit me and make me cry. That made me fear what else he might do.

One night I decided to change the playing field. I determined that I wouldn't let on that I was afraid. I stood my ground even though doing so would most likely put me in the position of being a punching bag. We had already broken up, and he had already moved out. Some of his things were still at my place. He came by one evening to ask me to help pick out an outfit for him to wear that evening. I just pushed the clothes that were hanging in my closet together and handed them to him. Well, that made him angry because I wasn't doing what he wanted. Apparently, he wanted just the one outfit, so he would have an excuse to come by another time to pick up some more of his clothes.

I didn't want him coming by again. He got really angry and got up in my face and began yelling at me and demanding that I do what he told me. I just stood there listening to him rave with a smile on my face. He asked if

I thought the situation was funny. I just kept smiling and suggested that he might want to ask me why I was smiling.

This took him aback. He asked, "What?" I stood my ground, still smiling, and repeated what I had just said. I was bluffing, big time, but he didn't know that. (Just for the record, I do not suggest anyone try this because it was not the smartest idea I ever had.)
I said, "I'm tired of you sticking your face in mine. Do you see that drawer right there?"
His gaze swiveled to the left, and he answered, "Yes."

"Do you know what's in it?" I asked. He took two steps backward away from me, picked up his clothes and started for the door. My refusal to show how afraid I was threw him off-balance. He had no idea how to respond nor what might happen. So, he left.

The same concept is shown throughout the Bible. Story after story tells of situations in which the Children of Israel were faced with armies that greatly outnumbered them. When they prayed to God for help and wisdom and direction, amazing, miraculous things happened. On one occasion, God instructed his people to send out the "praise team". When they looked, they were astonished to see that the enemy warriors had turned on themselves and were killing each other. The enemy knows that when praise goes up, the battle for right is already won.

Some of our battles will be won through praise; some will be won by the blood Christ shed, and some by the power of our testimonies. Trials and troubles will come—that's a fact. We cannot escape them. Jesus says, "In this world you will have trouble. But take heart; I have overcome the world." (John 16:23 NIV) Revelation 12:11 states that "They have overcome him (Satan) by the blood of the Lamb and by the word of their testimony…" (NIV)

In the account of the exodus of God's people from Egypt, Moses and the Israelites were caught between a rock (the Egyptian army) and a hard place, (actually a very wet place, as the Red Sea stood between them and freedom). What did Moses do? He prayed, of course. When God answered, He told Moses to stretch out his staff toward the Sea. When Moses obeyed, God sent a mighty wind that blew back the waves so the Israelites (about two million of them) could cross through the Red Sea on dry ground.

Everyone with Moses arrived safely on the other side. When the Egyptian army with its horses and chariots tried to chase them, God released the waters. The entire army was wiped out in one fell swoop.

There are many, many other examples of instances recorded in the Bible when God gave specific instructions to His people in order to save them from harm or disaster. Often God's way seemed foolish to those who heard it. But those who obeyed were rewarded with victory. He is asking us to trust Him on this journey. He is faithful; that is His nature. And He is all-powerful; there are no situations He cannot handle. When we build our lives on faith, our lives will change in ways that leave us in awe of God. I'm often amazed at His brilliance.

Proverbs 3: 5-6 states it clearly. "Trust in the Lord with all your heart and lean not on your own understanding; in all your ways acknowledge him and he will make your paths straight." (NIV)

Are we ready to know what Jesus knows, to see events through His eyes? As we learn to lean on Him, we'll grow spiritually while we walk through this journey called life.

Chapter Nine
Armed for Battle

As we all know, life is not a walk in the park. We are engaged in a battle, and to fight it based on our own understanding will certainly result in defeat. We're fighting against spiritual forces of evil in the heavenly realms, and we are no match for them.

The only way Satan's schemes and attacks can be defeated is for us to put on the armor of God. He has provided us with the defenses we need to wage the battle, but it is our responsibility to take them.

Ephesians 6:13-18 says, *"13 Therefore put on the full armor of God, so that when the day of evil comes, you may be able to stand your ground, and after you have done everything, to stand. 14 Stand firm the with the <u>belt of truth</u> buckled around your waist, with the <u>breastplate of righteousness</u> in place, 15 and with your <u>feet fitted with the readiness that comes from the gospel of peace.</u> 16 In addition to all this, take up the shield of faith, with which you can extinguish all the flaming arrows of the evil one. 17 Take the <u>helmet of salvation</u> and the <u>sword of the Spirit, which is the word of</u> God.*

Please notice that all the armor, except one, is defensive armor, designed to protect us. The only item of offense or attack is the Word of God.

Below are some scriptures that can guide us to better understanding: I encourage you to read them, not once, but several times. They are the words of life.

Jeremiah 29:11 "For I know the plans I have for you," declares the Lord, "plans to prosper you and not to harm you, plans to give you hope and a future."

1 Timothy 2:3-4 This is good, and pleases God our Savior, who wants all people to be saved and to come to a knowledge of truth.

1 Thessalonians 5:18 Give thanks in all circumstances; for this is God's will for you in Christ Jesus.

1Thessalonians 4:3 It is God's will that you should be sanctified; that you should avoid sexually immorality.

Hebrews 13:20-21 Now may the God of peace, who through the blood of the eternal covenant brought back from the dead our Lord Jesus Christ, that great Shepherd of the sheep, equip you with everything good for doing his will, and may he work in us what is pleasing to him, through Jesus Christ, to whom be glory forever and ever amen.

Luke 9:23 Then He said to them all, "Whoever wants to be my disciple must deny himself and take up his cross daily and follow me."

Psalm 119:105 Your word is a lamp for my feet, a light on my path.

James 1:5 If any of you lacks wisdom, you should ask God, who gives generously to all without finding fault, and it will be given to you.

1 Peter 2:15 For it is God's will that by doing good you should silence the ignorant talk of foolish people.

Ephesians 5:15-20 Be very careful, then, how you live-not as unwise but as wise, making the most of every opportunity, because the days are evil. Therefore, do not be foolish, but understand what the Lord's will is. Do not get drunk on wine which leads to debauchery. Instead, be filled with the Spirit, speaking to one another with psalms, hymns, and songs from the Spirit. Sing and make music from your heart to the Lord, always giving thanks to God the Father for everything, in the name of our Lord Jesus Christ.

Micah 6:8 He has shown you, O mortal, what is good. And what does the Lord require of you? To act justly and to love mercy and to walk humbly with your God.

Proverbs 16:4 The Lord works out everything to its proper end --- even the wicked for a day of disaster.

When others abuse us, the natural instinct is to get even. But this course of action does not honor God. Listen to the advice of King Solomon in Proverbs 25:21-22

If your enemy is hungry, give him food to eat; if he is thirsty, give him water to drink. In doing this, you will heap burning coals on his head. (NIV)

Kind of an unusual way to get even, isn't it? But being kind and forgiving to those who have hurt us honors God and prevents us from sinning. In the book of 1st Peter, Chapter 3, verse 9 we are encouraged not to repay evil with evil or insult with insult. When we respond in a loving way, we can walk away with a clear conscience.

When the opportunity comes to retaliate, and the temptation is strong, the Word encourages us to be slow to anger, slow to speak, and quick to listen to what the Holy Spirit is telling us to do. In other words, we need to think, even pray, before responding to abuse or insults. Slowing down and learning self-control will pay off in the long run, even if these actions and attitudes don't bring the instant gratification that we might be seeking.

It is also helpful for us to understand that the enemy knows us; he knows which "buttons" to push and how to push them to upset us. We are in training now and in the process of learning how to listen, not to our emotions, but to what the Spirit is leading us to do. Although, over time and with practice, it will become somewhat easier, the renewing of our minds through studying God's Word is a daily process. It's not a "once and done" sort of deal.

Our goal is to remember that our battles are not with people, although often that will seem to be the case. Satan introduces people into our situations who are difficult to deal with, people who try our souls and our patience, and people who are unkind and unfair. When we confront folks like this, we need to try to see beyond them and their actions to the key issues. There definitely is a battle going on, both here on earth and in the heavenly realms. When we come up against those who are obviously being used by Satan, the battles we fight will be won on our knees.

As we mentioned before, we are no match for Satan. But Jesus is. He has already defeated Satan by taking our sins upon Himself and paying the penalty once and for all. The actuality of the victory will be seen and felt when Satan is banished from the earth forever. Until then, we are caught up in the fray, and our best course of action is to follow His directives about how to deal with those who are in Satan's employ.

We need to search out the heart of Jesus in deciding what to do when Satan attacks. We must confess that we come to Him with a teachable mind and heart. We confess that the one who is in us is greater than the one who is in the world. (1 John 4:4) We claim the promise that no weapon formed against us will prosper and rebuke every accusation made against us. (Isaiah 54:17) <u>Saying the written Word of God has a power that is hard to imagine and impossible to refute.</u>

I encourage you to read Psalm 103 every day for at least two weeks. This is a bold statement about who God is and how He loves and treats His children.

Chapter Ten
The Baptism of the Holy Spirit

I'll never forget the day I received the baptism of the Holy Spirit. God had instructed me to begin attending church, but there were so many churches in town that I had no idea which one to choose. One day my sister-in-law invited me to go to church with her because some members of the family were being baptized. I felt that God must have told her to call, so I accepted.

During the praise and worship part of the service, a lady sitting in front of me began praying in the angelic tongue. I had never seen this before, so I got tickled and started to giggle. Tammy, my sister-in-law, noticed and quietly told me not to laugh. She said the lady was in the Spirit and was praying in a language I couldn't understand. When I asked why, Tammy smiled at me and said she would explain later and that I should relax and enjoy the service. I managed to control my urge to laugh.

Later, Tammy explained to me about the Holy Spirit and that the lady I heard was praying the perfect will of God. I asked why the lady had been crying, and Tammy explained that when someone is in the Spirit, he or she may sometimes laugh or cry. Some may even dance or run around when the anointing comes upon them. I realized then that I had a lot to learn.

Tammy invited me again the following Sunday. To be obedient to what I believed to be God's will, I again accepted. Before we were very far into the service, Tammy started praying in tongues, so I stood close to her and watched her. I asked Jesus what was going on with her because she was swaying and bowing as she prayed. Jesus told me that she was in His presence and was praying for the will of God

When Tammy started crying, I realized something special must be happening because I had never seen her cry before. Jesus told me to watch her face, so I did, and I could tell that where she was must be really amazing because she had a totally different look on her face. My words cannot truly describe the beautiful flow between heaven and earth that was going on that day. The more I was in that atmosphere, the more I desired such an intimate relationship with God, the Father, and God, the Son. That is one of the main services of the Holy Spirit—to call us to the other Persons in the Trinity.

That day, when the pastor issued the altar call, I went forward. But before the pastor could get to me, I felt the presence of the Holy Spirit come upon me, and I was filled with Him. I had intended to remain standing, but could not. I fell to the floor and lay there on my back looking up at the ceiling. Then I felt Jesus kneel next to me. This event happened when I was still new in my journey and had not yet been able to forgive myself for all the wrong choices I had made. There was still so much pain in my heart. As I lay there, unable to get up, I heard Jesus say, "I love you."

This broke my heart; all I could manage to say between the tears was, "How could you love me?" My sins had hurt Him so much! How could He love me?

Again He said the words, "I love you." He repeated them over and over until my questions stopped. At some point, I felt His love fill my heart. My whole body felt His presence and his love, and I lay there for an indeterminate length of time, in the safe and loving presence of Jesus.

For the first time in my life I knew what pure love felt like. My heart, after pouring out all the hurt and pain, was finally ready to receive it. Tears of joy flowed down my cheeks. I felt consumed with overwhelming love. Words cannot adequately express what the highest and deepest love of God feels like. We must experience it.

> Father, I ask that all those who are called by your name be able to experience your love. I ask this in Jesus' name, and I thank you in advance because I know you will. You are amazing, and I praise you and honor you, Lord Jesus, for all you have done and will do. Thank you with all my heart. I love you Jesus, Father God, and Holy Spirit.

Jesus declares the extent of His love for us in John 15:9 where He says, "As the Father has loved me, so have I loved you. Remain in my love." (NIV)

I speak blessings over each of you that you may know the love of God. I believe this is a good place to pray over you what Paul prayed in Ephesians 3:14-19.

For this reason I kneel before the Father, from whom his whole family in heaven and on earth derives its name. I pray that out of his glorious riches he may strengthen you with power through his Spirit in your inner being, so that Christ may dwell in your hearts through faith. And I pray that you, being rooted and established in love, may have power, together with all the saints, to grasp how wide and long and high and deep is the love of Christ, and to know this love that surpasses knowledge—that you may be filled to the measure of all the fullness of God.

Isn't that a beautiful prayer? What we need to do now is to learn to personalize what we read in Scripture. A major part in the renewing of our minds in Christ Jesus is to become confident that the promises are ours. In beginning to understand the depth of His love for us, we can thank Him that His love isn't conditional as man's love is. The love God has for us isn't based on our behavior or how good or bad we are.

The Bible says that God is love, itself. It is His nature. And we thank Him for that! Not a single one of us deserves the kind of love that God has for us, the kind of love that would allow sinful men to nail God's own precious son to a Cross to die in our stead. But it is our responsibility to receive it. His love is offered to all, but not everyone will admit the need for a Savior. Learning to trust is, like our journey to recovery, a one-step-at-a-time proposition. We will probably take baby steps at first. We may even backslide or be plagued by doubts. But God doesn't change, and His love for us remains constant.

Chapter Eleven
Facing the Past

Most of us have experienced some pretty rough times in our lives. We may very well ask where God was during those times. If He loved me, why did He allow me to go through so much pain? No one can answer that. God sees the big picture; we don't.

What I do understand now is that God has been with me throughout my life. His promise is that He will never leave us nor forsake us, although there have probably been times when each of us has felt forsaken.

I felt His presence and His direction after I turned my life over to Him. For example, when I was trying to explain to my daughters why I had made some of the poor choices I had made, God told me to stop trying. My attempts were only making matters worse. I wanted to make things better for them, but in reality, I couldn't. God told me to stop because I couldn't see or know what Satan had already done in their lives. God told me to give my daughters to Him, that He was the only one who could heal them.

I fought with God over control of my children. I felt like I was abdicating my responsibility to them. And I sure didn't need more guilt in my life. That was the wrong mindset. I needed for God to allow me to see through His eyes so that after a while I was able to trust Him with my daughters' lives.

But I still had a huge question that I needed to have an answer to. I asked God what I had done to deserve all the negative things I had happened to me in my life. Instead of answering, He asked me a question. Are you ready to hear His response? He asked, "What choices did you make that would ensure that you would not experience those things?" He put it back on me! Please understand that I was asking about situations that occurred in my adult life, not those that occurred during my childhood. I had no say in the things that happened within my family; I was a child. But when I became an adult, the choices I made were mine, and they had consequences, not only for me, but for my daughters and family, as well.

As I progressed in my journey, God would sometimes show me a slide show of things that had happened in my past to prepare me for the season He was bringing me into. We have seasons of revealing and repentance and seasons of healing and forgiveness. I didn't know God or His ways very well; all I had to lean on was my own understanding. Some of you will experience these seasons, as well.

I want you to understand that we are always free to ask God questions. He's very well aware that we don't know the answers. In the beginning I had so many more questions than answers. So, please don't hesitate to tell God what you need help with and ask Him for the answers. You see, this journey is about being real and not pretending that everything is all right. We have nothing to hide from God. It wouldn't do any good if we did, because He knows us in our innermost parts. He knows our thoughts and our fears and our motives. I decided not to try to hide anything because I wanted freedom. I desired to know the truth, and I was determined to find it.

As God began to allow the pictures of the past that flashed quickly before my eyes, I thought He was being mean to me. I asked Him. I had lived through it once and couldn't understand why He would put me through it again, even in my memories. I didn't understand why God would take me back, mentally, to those places where I had been beaten and raped and cursed at—where I was constantly being told what a horrible person I was. More than once these memories would have me in tears again. It was never my plan to be no more than a punching bag to someone, just someone to take care of his house while he went off to do whatever he wanted to do with whomever he wanted to do it.

While I was living like that, I fell deeper and deeper into sin. Staying in an abusive relationship, making one poor choice after another, amounted to one long, wrong choice. Finally, I ended those kinds of relationships once and for all. There were so many things God wanted to teach me, but we don't learn everything we need to know all at once. Like everything else, it's bit by bit, one step at a time.

In order to be prepared for our journey, we need to understand that we shouldn't run from whatever it is in our past that God brings to mind, nor to press it back down. We need to allow God to walk with us through those events. When God spoke to me, He said, "I did not show you any of your past in order to hurt you, little one, but to reveal the truth so that you might be set free."

The path to truth is built by accepting the fact that what we once believed to be true was not. As we mentioned before, we must stop seeing other people as the enemy and come to understand that while Satan was using them to hurt others, they, themselves were being hurt in the process.

God told me that there were two things I needed to do in the beginning of my journey to truth and freedom. The first one was to forgive so that I might be forgiven. I was willing to learn how to forgive because I needed for those I had hurt to forgive me. That was both for my sake and for theirs. They couldn't be healed until they were able to forgive, too. We understand that we cannot force someone to forgive us nor blame them if they can't or won't. That is in God's providence. We need to let go and let God do His part while we concentrate on the strategy He has outlined for us.

The other aspect I was to focus on was learning not to fear. Once I could concentrate on holding on to these two tenets, I was ready to answer the question God had asked me when I asked him what I had done to deserve all the cruel, abusive and seemingly unfair things that had happened to me. I had to take an honest look at my choices, and <u>I could not face them if I feared knowing the truth.</u> This is a very powerful statement that I hope you will write down and say to yourself over and over while we travel down this path.

Fear will not allow us to see and accept the truth because fear is a prison cell, designed to keep us in bondage. Fear is a weapon that Satan uses to keep us under his thumb. The opposite stance to walking in fear is to walk in faith. As we walk in faith, one step at a time, we learn to accept and understand that God has our best interests at heart. When I could look at my past honestly, I came to acknowledge the fact that, when faced with decisions, I never invited God into the decision-making process. When we leave God and His wisdom and His will out of the equation, how can we expect positive results? In the fifteenth chapter of John, Jesus tells us that apart from Him we can do nothing. But when we abide in Him and He abides in us, we can do all things through His strength.

Chapter Twelve
Thoughts and Words

The next verse we need to consider when making decisions is one we can use as a weapon against the wiles of Satan. Remember, when we were talking about the full armor of God, that the only weapon was the sword of the Sprit, which is the Word of God. In John 8:44, Jesus is speaking to the Pharisees who are challenging His claim that He is the Son of God.

> *You belong to your father, the devil, and you want to carry out you father's desires. He was a murderer from the beginning, not holding to the truth, for there is no truth in him. When he lies, he speaks his native language, for he is a liar and the father of lies. (NIV)*

From the beginning of time Satan has used deception to play with our minds. Just as he spoke half-truths to Eve in the Garden of Eden, he does the same with us. He begins by whispering some word in our ears that sounds like truth. We might believe these thoughts are coming from our own minds, but we are being deceived. We should pray for discernment, to test what we're hearing. Ask yourself, "Does this thought line up with the Word of God?"

Here is what Scripture says regarding this battle:

2 Corinthians 10:3-6, For though we live in the world, we do not wage war as the world does. The weapons we fight with are not the weapons of the world. On the contrary, they have divine power to demolish strongholds. We demolish arguments and every pretension that sets itself up against the knowledge of God, and we take captive every thought to make it obedient to Christ. And we will be ready to punish every act of disobedience, once your obedience is complete. (NIV)

This scripture shows us that our thoughts matter just as much and the words we speak.

Have you ever considered what you're actually thinking about? What thoughts are you entertaining in your mind? Joyce Meyers has written a book titled, The Battlefield of the Mind. If you haven't read it, I earnestly suggest that you find a copy and read it. We can understand that our journey encompasses so many aspects that we can only take it one step at a time, and each step is taken by faith. But it is even more important to recognize that our faith is in God, not man, nor in situations and circumstances.

Second Corinthians tells us, "So we fix our eyes not on what is seen, but what is unseen. For what is seen is temporary, but what is unseen is eternal." Anything we can see is subject to change, but eternal things remain fixed and constant.

And it's all about faith and about believing God's promises to us.
> Therefore, the promise comes by faith…not only to those who are of the law, but also to those who are of the faith of Abraham. He is the father of us all. Romans 4:16

If Abraham had looked only at his circumstances, he would not have believed God. He was 75 years old when God first spoke to him, (his name was Abram at the time) and told him that through his offspring the whole world would be blessed. But Abram had to wait in faith for twenty-five years, knowing all the while that he was growing older by the day, and so was Sarai, his childless wife. He was ninety-nine years old when God changed his name from Abram to Abraham, which meant "father of many nations," and gave him the son of promise.

Neither his age nor his body nor the fact that his wife was barren caused him to doubt that God would deliver on His promise. He didn't look at his circumstances; his focus was on the character and power of God.

So, when we want to invite God's will and His plan into our lives, let's do it. Begin to claim as blessings the things that happen in your life. Jesus came that we might have an abundant life in Him.

Our words also have the power to produce fruit. We must choose to speak life and stop allowing foolish words to form in our mouths. We are the only ones who can decide what comes out of our mouths. If our hearts are right with God, our speech will be, too. The Bible tells us that, "out of the overflow of the heart, the mouth speaks." Luke 6:45(b)

I'm not saying this is easy. But we can do all things through the strength of the Son of God. Trust me when I tell you that when we try to do anything through our own strength and abilities, we will surely fall short.

Nor can we blame other people for our failures and shortcomings. We should not be watching the actions of others to justify how we are acting or what we are saying. God won't buy that. It won't work for us any more than it worked for Adam and Eve in the Garden. When God called for Adam, He already knew where he was and what he had done. God didn't ask the questions He voiced to Adam to find out anything. He already knew what the answer was going to be. As He did with Adam, He asks us questions to call us to account.

It's possible that He asked Adam what he had done to give him the chance to own up to his sins. Instead, Adam blamed first, his wife, and then God, for giving him a wife in the first place.

God always knows the truth because He IS truth. If we answer "yes" when we ask ourselves if we believe we'll always have all the strength we'll need to get through anything life throws at us, we are deceiving ourselves and being prideful. And a fall in certainly in the offing. Either God will bring us to our knees, or the world will. Believing that our thoughts are more impressive than God's or that our ways are just as good as His is tantamount to opening the door to Satan. It was pride and ambition that led to Satan's expulsion from Heaven, and God will not allow us to live very long in pride. When the fall comes, He will allow it. He will suffer with us and be patient with us and give us time and opportunity to repent, but most likely, He won't disrupt the inevitable results of our pride.

Important scriptures:

> Galatians 6:7-10 Be not deceived; God is not mocked: for whats ever a man soweth, that shall he also reap.8 For he that soweth to his flesh shall of the flesh reap corruption; but he that soweth to the Spirit shall of the Spirit reap life everlasting.9 And let us not be weary in well-doing: for in due season we shall reap, if we faint not. (10) As we have therefore opportunity, let us do good unto all men, especially unto them who are of the household of faith. (KJV)

I suggest you read the whole chapter in Galatians 6 to help you know the ways of God.

We need to begin each day of our journey with a time of praise. We can thank Jesus for what He's already done for us and for being the way, the truth, and the life. We can praise Him for being obedient to the Father, even to the point of death. We can thank Him for going to Hell for us so that we don't have to. We can thank Him for the salvation he offers us by grace. There is nothing we can do to earn this gift. Because of His shed blood, we can stand before the throne of God, not as sinners, but clothed in the righteousness of His Son.

And He gives us a job to do, a calling found in Isaiah 42:6-7
> *I, the Lord, have called you in righteousness; I will take hold of your hand. I will keep you and will make you to be a covenant for the people, to open the eyes that are blind, to free captives from prison, and to release from the dungeon those who sit in darkness.*

Chapter Thirteen
Transformed: Flesh vs. Spirit

Do not conform to the pattern of this world, but be transformed by the renewing of your mind. Then you will be able to discern and approve what Gods will is. Romans 12:2

To begin with, it is important that we learn to discern the difference between thoughts and actions that are under the control of fleshly desires and those that are controlled by the Spirit. Fleshly desires are those which involve lust of some sort: sex, appetite, control, power, money, comfort, luxuries, even popularity and the desire for acceptance and acclaim can be considered "lusts" if they impel us to satisfy them.

Romans 8: 5-8 teaches us that those who live according to the sinful nature have their minds set on what that nature desires; but those who live in accordance with the Spirit have their minds set on what the Spirit desires.

The mind of sinful man is death, but the mind controlled by the Spirit is life and peace; the sinful mind is hostile to God. It does not submit to God's law, nor can it do so. Those controlled by the sinful nature cannot please God.

If we are going through our days attempting to gratify the lusts of the flesh, we are apart from the will of God, and His nature is not dominant in our lives and choices.

Do you remember when we talked about how I asked God what I had done to deserve the negative events of my life? The answer is simple, and

and it's found in the verses mentioned above. Those who sow to the flesh will reap corruption. That means, friends, that we reap what we sow. I had been planting seeds of fleshly desires, and I had reaped the natural consequences of those actions. In short, I had not been living my life according to its original design. The result was 'corruption" and was an example of a life lived without Christ.

It's hard to admit, but Jesus wasn't controlling my thoughts and actions; Satan was. I was buying into his lies because I had not met the alternative, Jesus. John 10:10 reports that "the thief comes only to steal, kill and destroy," but Jesus comes "that they might have life and have it to the full." Satan wants to rob us of everything that is, or should be, important to us—our joy, our purpose, our sense of fulfillment, our ability to love and be loved, healthy relationships, etc. We can expect an impoverished life when we live according the Satan's plan, But choosing God's way leads to eternal life, and that life begins the moment we put Him on the throne of our lives where He belongs.

The purpose of our journey is to draw us closer to God, Jesus, and the Holy Spirit. We must learn to stand on the truth, to hold onto it tightly, and not be moved or persuaded by others or through the enemy's deceitful wiles. I pray that in the midst of our journey that we grow stronger and wiser.

I strongly suggest you read the fourth chapter of James. In fact, you might want to read the whole book of James. It is just a few pages long, and in it you will find practical advice for ways to walk the walk that is pleasing to God. In fact, throughout the Bible we come to understand that God is revealing to us truths about His Kingdom.

In Colossians 1:9-14 Paul, in this letter to Colossae, prays that they might be filled with the knowledge of His will in wisdom and spiritual understanding, so that they might walk in a manner worthy of the Lord, pleasing Him and being fruitful, strengthened by the power of God, being patient and giving thanks to the Father.

God has qualified us to have a part in His inheritance and has delivered us from the power of darkness through the sacrifice of His Son.

Chapter Fourteen
Sowing the Seed

Throughout much of our discussion we have talked about the kind of seeds we sow, whether to fulfill the desires of the flesh or to sow to the Spirit. In the following parable, Jesus talks about what happens when the seed of the Word of God is sown. It doesn't all take root and flourish. I'm sure He was aware, when He spoke to hundreds and thousands of people who came out to hear Him, that the spirit life of some of them would be blessed beyond measure, while some would walk away unchanged.

In the eighth chapter of the book of Luke, Jesus recounts a story about a farmer who goes out into his fields to plant his seed. The method he used was one that was employed by many in that era. He simply put his seed in a bag and grabbed a handful of seed and flung it out onto the field as he walked.

Some of the seeds fell on the path where the ground was packed hard because it had been trampled on, and the birds came and snatched it up. Some fell on rocky (gravel) soil, and although it sprang up quickly, there was not enough soil beneath it to hold water and allow it to take root. Other seeds fell among thorns and weeds, which grew along with the seed as it came up and soon choked the tender young plants. But other seeds fell on good soil. They sprouted and thrived and produced a hundred-fold crop.

When Jesus spoke in parables, He incorporated His message into stories, using illustrations that almost everyone who heard Him could relate to. After telling the parable of the seeds, he called out, "He who has ears to hear, let him hear." What He's saying here is, "Are you listening? Do you have ears? Then pay attention to what I'm saying!"

Even the disciples didn't understand, and when they were alone with Him, they asked for an explanation.

Luke 8; 11-15 gives us this explanation of the parable.

> The "seed" is the Word of God.
> Those people who are on the beaten path are the ones who hear, but their hearts are hardened, and the devil comes and takes the word away from them. Unfortunately, this happens far too often.
>
> Those people whose hearts are like the gravelly soil are the ones who receive the message with joy, but there is no soil underneath, so the seed cannot take root. They may believe for a while, but in the time of testing, they fall away.
>
> The seeds that fell among the thorns refer to the hearts of those who receive the Word, but the concerns and cares and pleasures of life soon overwhelm them, and the Word is choked out.
>
> But some of the seed fell on good soil; good soil refers to the hearts of those who are noble and good. There, the Word takes root and produces fruit, up to one hundred times more than what was received.

In the lives of those who stay the course in faith, the Word produces the fruit of the Spirit for them to share with others.

People can read the Bible and listen to the Word of God, while missing the clear instructions that show us how to be fruitful. The Word tells us that we can know people by the fruit they are producing. If we are abiding in the Word, and God is abiding in us, the Spirit will produce fruit in from our lives in keeping with God's will and nature.

It is so important to spend time in the Word, asking God to speak to us through it. He is speaking to us all the time. We need to develop spiritual "ears" to allow us to hear what He is saying. All our communications with Him help enable the seed of His word to grow in our lives.

It will help us in our walk if we remember to journal what we hear and what we've discovered along the way. We need to write down our prayers so that later we can look back and see how He's answered them. This habit will help us to maintain an "attitude of gratitude" as we recognize that God is answering. When His answer is "no," we may later understand why that was the best answer for us at that time.

We may think that God is more concerned with our time on earth than our eternal destination. Is He more concerned with the level of our comfort, or the salvation and sanctification of our souls? I can guarantee you that not every part of our journey will be fun. Much of it will be hard, and there will undoubtedly be days when we may want to stop and cry "uncle".

There will be moments when the pressure will grow intense. Those are the moments when we are in the refining fire. Those times when our flesh wants to throw in the towel are the moments when we are experiencing the act of "dying to ourselves." We will come to recognize when we are being controlled by the desires of the flesh. We will grow wiser as we begin to see that it is the carnal part of us that is dictating whether we are sad, depressed, confused, disappointed, or feeling rejected or offended.

We were not designed to be controlled by these feelings. We were designed by the same Creator who spoke light into the universe. When He created mankind, He breathed His own breath into him so he became a living being.

As we seek to know Him better and pray for wisdom through the renewing of our minds, our lives will begin to change. We will learn not to evaluate our lives in terms of days, week, months and years. We walk in faith, moment by moment. When we remind ourselves that Satan will bombard us with life's cares, the lure of riches, and the incitement of pleasures in an attempt to draw us away from abiding in God, we can concentrate more fully on allowing the seed of His Word to produce the harvest He intends.

One day I was really angry at God for what He was revealing to me. Then He asked me a question, "What is the root of your anger?" That's an important question. We can feel the anger, but often we don't take the time to delve more deeply and understand what is causing it. The anger is only the tip of the iceberg, so to speak. It is what we feel, but often we don't address the root causes that lie beneath the surface. Am I angry because I didn't get my own way? Is it because I don't want to face my responsibility in what happened? Is it because I don't want to give up control of my life? Is it because I want to hang on to thought patterns and life choices that do not honor God?

We might compare this type of situation with mowing a lawn. From a distance, everything looks green, and the weeds mixed in with the grass don't show. When we mow the lawn, we just skim off the top layer. When the grass looks uniform, we are seeing only the surface. We don't see the weeds, and cutting the tops off of them will not reveal their roots. Now the question we need to answer is this: Did we get to the root of the problem (weeds) just by mowing over them? Or is it only the appearance that changed? Now what we need to consider is this: Did we, just by mowing over the weed, remove the whole weed, or did it just look like we did? To find a solution to the problem we will need to get past the surface to the root.

Our walk with Christ is similar, and we often have to get past several layers to get to the root of our negative emotions. Sometimes those roots go deep; sometimes we'd rather not go "digging" at all.

Whatever the root sources of our emotions, we need to find the root causes and deal with them. And I strongly urge you, when you feel these negative emotions, not to allow them to persuade you to quit on the journey. We still face trials. That's a given. Jesus even says that "In this world you will have troubles, but take heart, I have overcome the world." (John 16:33, NIV)

In his book, the apostle, James, guides us to a new way of thinking about life's difficulties in Chapter 1, verses 2-5, He says we are to "Consider it joy, my brothers, when you face trials of many kinds, because you know that the testing of your faith develops perseverance. Perseverance must finish its work so that you may be mature and complete, not lacking anything. If any of you lack wisdom, he should ask God, who gives generously to all without finding fault, and it will be given him. But when we ask, we must believe and not doubt, because the one who doubts is like a wave of the sea, blown and tossed by the wind. That person should not expect to receive anything from the Lord. Such a person is double-minded and unstable in all they do."

Just as our physical muscles will not grow strong without challenging them, neither will our faith. Faith that is untried will not stand up under pressure.

Chapter Fifteen
Getting to the Roots

The things that happen to us, the things we see and hear, can create moods and reactions in us. Our feelings are nearly always at or near the surface, and we're very aware of them. If we just accept negative emotions without trying to discover their roots, they tend to stay where they are. And "mowing over" them only allows the roots to grow deeper and take a more tenacious hold.

I remember an incident that occurred in the work place that made me angry. A person over whom I had authority did not do what was asked. My leadership role made me responsible for getting the work accomplished, and when those under me didn't follow instructions, the job didn't get done. Those under me didn't seem to understand that I would "write up" their negative behaviors. Even though I sometimes felt like I needed to do a better job of applying incentives and setting boundaries, their refusal to carry their end of the load was making me very angry.

I asked God to show me why this type of situation angered me so much. God led me to the understanding that my anger was the surface issue, not the root. Just like businesses have procedures and protocols that, when followed, lead to increased productivity, God's Kingdom also has an order, or design, to it that allows for growth and maturity. When God asked me to try to understand the root of my anger, I was at a loss. So, I asked for help. He showed me that the root of my anger was fear.

That surprised me. I asked God how fear could be the root of anger. And how could fear make me lose my composure? What was I afraid of? To answer that, I had to ask myself some questions. Exactly what, in that situation, made me the angriest? If I removed the "layer" that concerned the way my co-workers acted, the way they refused to listen to me, I had to ask myself why that made me angry. The same thing applies to when our children don't obey; we can get angry to the point of yelling.

Fear has many faces. We may fear the unknown; fear the unexpected; fear losing control, over ourselves and others; fear losing the respect we feel we deserve, etc. God showed me that the root of anger is fear. Think about this; if we believe we have control over a situation, we will not fear the outcome. Fear often puts the face of reality on something that isn't real at all.

When we take off the layers of anger, we break it down to fear. Then we can face our fears one by one. Remember that Jesus said, "You shall know the truth, and the truth will set you free." That's why we need to learn to be absolutely honest with ourselves and with God. And when we feel angry, we need to write down what situation made us angry and figure out what it is we are afraid of. What unknown outcome can cause us to be anxious? We can invite God into this search and ask Him to reveal hidden truths that may be hard to come by.

Be sure to write your experiences down so you will have them to refer to at a later time.

We may try with our carnal minds to ferret out the truth behind our anger, but in our carnal minds is not where we want to stay. Why? Romans 8:7 tells us that "the carnal (sinful) mind is hostile to God. It does not submit to God's laws, nor can it do so." We can save ourselves a lot of time in over-thinking this matter, or we can do the smart thing and ask the Holy Spirit to reveal the truth to us. Remember what we said? We shall know the truth and the truth will set us free. And God has promised to give wisdom to those who ask without judging, whether or not we deserve it.

When God finally revealed to me what the root of my anger was, I sat there trying to wrap my mind around the fact that my anger was rooted in fear. Anger usually acts itself out in words and actions. We may very well sin when we are angry. The Bible doesn't say it is wrong to be angry; in fact we would be less than human if we never got angry. Jesus, Himself, became angry at times. But it does caution us to be careful not to allow anger to cause us to sin.

In the situation I mentioned earlier, the root cause of my anger was the fear of failure. I could not have understood that if I hadn't been willing to receive the truth in wisdom. The spirit of fear is often the result of Satan's strategy to keep us deceived. Therefore, we must continually renew our minds in God because He has not given us a spirit of fear. Plainly stated, we can be sure that if we're feeling afraid, that spirit didn't come from God.

He tells us that we can do all things through His strength. For example, raising children can be frustrating, discouraging, and just plain hard. When we come up against difficult situations in parenting, if our children refuse to listen to us or obey us, we can be encouraged because we can ask for help from Jesus. We can invite Him into our situation. We are invited to come boldly before the throne of grace to obtain mercy and find help in our times of need. We can ask the Holy Spirit to give us the words we need to speak and that others need to hear. If we ask, he will teach us how we can walk by faith. One of the fruits of the Spirit is patience, and we will need a lot of it during our walk.

Chapter Sixteen
Denying Ourselves

One of the biggest challenges I have faced on this journey was learning why and how to deny myself. I had grown so accustomed to trusting myself that when I began the process of renewing my mind, it felt strange. I remember driving to work one morning, quoting the Word of God. It felt strange hearing myself talk like that, but I pressed on and continued. Still, to this day I speak the Word of God.

Jesus says in Luke 9:23 that, "If any man would come after me, he must deny himself and take up his cross daily, and follow me." Denying ourselves daily is an important part of our new journey. We will have moments when our flesh will rear up and demand attention. I recall the morning I was sitting in Sunday school class. Something unusual was going on in my spirit and my "self" wanted to be verbal about what I was experiencing. My teacher, Ramona, noticed the struggle I was having and came over to me and asked if I was all right. I looked up at her with tears in my eyes and shook my head. I said, "No, and I don't know how to explain it."

She encouraged me to try, so I looked at her, feeling like I was about to fall apart, and replied, "I have come to the end of me."

She smiled at me and asked if I had been denying myself and following Jesus, whereupon I nodded my head. She patted my leg and said, "Honey, you are in a good place. Let's pray for you." She began praying as the Holy Spirit poured Himself into me. When I sensed His power, I felt so much better.

One lesson I've learned on my journey is that dying to oneself is something that we have to do on a daily basis. Paul said that it wasn't he who lived, but Christ who lived in him. John the Baptist said that he must decrease and Christ must increase. That means we must live our lives in the shadow and by the power and Spirit of the Almighty.

I realized that the reason I was feeling so sad was because the fleshly, or carnal, part of me was dying, and I had to tell my old "self" good-bye. But this is good for us and for the Kingdom. We need to give the earthly part of us a burial and move forward in the Spirit.

Yes, this can be painful, but the consequences are worth the pain. The stronger our desire to say good-bye to the carnal nature, the closer we are to reaching the goal line.

Chapter Seventeen
Paying It Forward

To illustrate this, let's look at a true story of a coach that God had been calling into the ministry and what God showed him. God can, and often does, show us the ways of the Kingdom by using the things of the natural world.

In this account, God asked the coach what the hardest yard on the football grid was to make. The coach responded, "The last yard before the goal line." Why was the one-yard line the hardest to make? From the point of view of the defense, the goal is to keep the offense from scoring by whatever means they can—tackling, intercepting the football, sacking the quarterback, etc.

While the coach was in the Spirit, God took him to a football game; they were sitting in the stands. The coach could smell the popcorn and hot dogs. When he asked God what they were doing there, God told him to watch the game. In the coach's mind, that was "all good." He loved football.

Then God moved them to seats on the fifty-yard line. The coach really liked these seats. As they watched, the coach realized that the team they were watching was the same one he had played on in high school. He was, in essence, watching himself play the game as a receiver. The coach was thinking that he sure hoped they were watching one of his best games.

He and God stood watching the game. He, as the receiver, was wide open, no defensive players around him. The quarterback threw the ball to him, and he caught the football. But instead of running with the ball, he "took a knee." The crowd and his teammates were screaming at him. When the players returned to the huddle, the quarterback asked him if he knew what his job was. He replied, "I am a receiver. My job is to catch the ball. I did that. I did my job."

The quarterback answered with another question. "Do you know what the "er" at the end of receiver means? It stands for "extra responsibility." Once you receive the ball, you have an additional responsibility to advance the ball, to make progress with what you have received."

At that point, God asked the coach if he had received the word of God. Of course, the coach replied, "Yes, I guess I have." Then he realized what God was wanting him to understand. The coach had been fighting the call of God to preach the gospel.

All at once, still in the Spirit, God and the coach were standing at the goal line. His team was on the one-yard line, and he was waiting to see if his team scored a touchdown. At that moment, the coach heard the most awful sounds coming from the field. Instead of uniformed football players on the field, there were men and women crying, while demons were screaming at them to give up—they would never make it.

God's voice couldn't be heard above the din of the screaming demons, and the people were repeating what they heard the demons saying. Things like…
"I can't do it!"
"I quit!"
"Why me, Lord?"

All the coach could see on the field were people who had been wounded, like on a battlefield. The sights and sounds were more than the coach could take. He turned to God and asked why God was showing him this disturbing sight.

With tears in His eyes, God replied, "These are my people. They had made it all the way to the one-yard line. Then the enemy sent out the big demons to attack them. The people had come as far as they could on their own power; then they quit. God told the coach to look at the people. They were all wounded, every one of them, and some had been wounded by "friendly" fire.

When the coach asked the Lord what friendly fire was, God told him the friendly fire that had hurt them had come from people in the churches—

from other Christians. They had been wounded and left on the battlefield, and nobody would go out to pick them up, bring them in, bind their wounds and heal them.

God said he hated that. His people must do something with what they receive in His Word. They need to help each other to accomplish the journey together as the unified body of Christ.

Christians have received the Word of God, and we all have the "e-r"…the extra responsibility… to share what we have received—to help others when we see them struggling, to lift each other up in prayer, and to encourage each other. Believing, praying Christians are always a threat to the enemy, but our threat increases when we apply the Word of God.

When we pray and "pass it on," Satan tries to stop us. We can expect to be hit hard with temptation to doubt what we believe. He wants to stop us by making us think we can't go any further. It helps to understand that this is what is happening and to see that we are in a battle. When we cross over the goal line and help others do so, the angels in heaven rejoice. I like to call it the "glory goal." Our strength to do this does not come from ourselves, but from Christ who strengthens us in all things.

I have a goal-line story, too. When my daughter was eighteen, she became very sick, to the point that she could not walk, and any kind of movement was painful. I had taken her to the doctor three times, but she didn't improve. In fact, each day, she became more and more ill. When I wanted to take her back to the doctor, she wasn't even able to walk to the car. I asked someone to help me push her in a chair to the car and help me to get her into the car.

I was determined that this time I was not leaving the emergency room until they had admitted her. My heart was racing, and fear was threatening to overwhelm me. I kept talking to Jesus. The doctor finally admitted her, asking what was wrong. Her legs began to swell, and, of course, she couldn't walk. When I looked into her eyes and saw the fear there-- the look of all the "what if's" she was imagining, my heart clinched up tightly.

I hated being in the place, spiritually, where fear was getting the upper hand. And I hated that this was happening to her. She was going downhill. The swelling in her feet was so bad and painful that I could not even touch her. We needed help, fast! What the tests revealed was that she had a major staph infection. They hooked up an I.V of antibiotics so strong that they burned her veins..

All the while I was praying and believing that she would be healed. After seven days, the swelling was diminishing, and her body began, gradually, to return to normal. When she was recovered sufficiently that we could leave the hospital, the doctor cautioned us to be on our guard. He said to bring her back to the hospital if she appeared to be getting even a cold or if her eyes started watering.

My daughter had been living with a friend, so when she was released from the hospital, she went back out to their home thirty miles away.

A few weeks later, my daughter called me again while I was at work and told me she hadn't been feeling well and was going to the doctor. As any mother's heart would do, mine began to race, fearing a recurrence of our previous episode. I told myself to calm down and trust God. I asked her to call me as soon as she saw the doctor.

I didn't hear from her again until I was off work and back at home. When she finally did call, I could tell that she was crying. My heart was screaming, "What is wrong? What did the doctors say? Are you in the hospital?"

She just kept on crying while my imagination was running away with me. I took a deep breath, asking God to help me, to prepare me for what I was about to hear. She asked me not to be upset with her, and I promised I wouldn't. But I needed to know what was wrong. It was then that she told me she was pregnant. My mind raced with all kinds of thoughts, but the Lord told me to choose my words very carefully, because what I said at that moment would stay with her for the rest of her life.

My emotions were swirling as I stood there in my dining room, holding the phone in my hand, thankful that I had the counter to hold on to. Coincidentally, it was the same counter I had been holding on to the day I came to Jesus.

I listened, searching for wisdom about how to respond to my daughter's announcement. I mumbled a few words while my daughter was silent on the other end of the line. The Lord directed me to encourage her and con gratulate her and ask her for time to process this news. With obvious relief in her voice, she said, "Sure."

Several months after my granddaughter was born, I was on my way to work, when my daughter called again. She told me she was hurting and throwing up, and the pain wouldn't stop. She asked me, once again, if I could take her to the E.R.

My job at the time was managing a fast-food restaurant, and I was the one who was supposed to open up that morning. I spent the time during the thirty-mile drive to pick up my daughter calling people to try to find someone to fill in for me. No one answered the phone. When I arrived at my daughter's apartment, I discovered that she had asked a friend to watch the baby, so we left immediately.

While we were driving to the hospital, I told her not to worry, that I would find someone to work my shift. I left her there and headed across town to my job. In spite of all my efforts to find a replacement, no one would agree to come in. I knew that, unless I could get someone to cover my shift, I couldn't leave. At that moment I felt like no one cared about me or my daughter or the situation we were in.

One of my daughter's friends came to stay with her in the E.R and called me regularly with updates. The doctors were running tests, and so far they'd been unable to find out what was wrong. When I explained to the friend that I had been unable to find anyone to work my shift, I could hear in her voice that she thought I should have been at the hospital, regardless. Her attitude made me question what kind of mother I was—putting my job before my daughter's welfare.

But that's what single parents sometimes have to do. I felt like I was on the football field, and the whole defensive team was coming at me from all sides. It was then that I reached the point that I had had enough. I had been praying and asking for help, but hadn't received any answers. So I told God that I needed Him to tell me one good reason why I shouldn't take the store keys off my belt and walk out. It was at that moment that I heard Him say, "You are there!" I loosened the grip on my keys and said, "What?"

The Lord repeated what he had just said, "You are there." I knew exactly what He was referring to. I was at the goal line. Was I going to quit and let the enemy win? Or was I going for the goal? As soon as I had made the choice not to quit my job, the phone rang. My daughter was on the other end of the line. She told me that all of a sudden, her pains and nausea had left, and she felt fine. The doctors hadn't found anything wrong with her, so she had gone back home.

I praised Jesus and thanked him for helping me understand the situation. All I had to do to cross the goal line and score a victory was to trust God and to resist the forces of Satan.

Many of our choices hold life and death in them. I am so thankful for the wisdom to be obedient. I'm thankful that He opened the eyes of understanding and gave me the enlightenment I needed to know the ways and thoughts of God. It was positive proof that if we seek first HIS Kingdom and HIS righteousness, that everything else will be provided.

AUTHOR'S NOTE:

I'm so thankful for the men and women who lay down their lives so that others may know the life we can find in Christ.

And I thank you for taking this journey with me. I hope it has helped you in some way to find the path to peace and understanding. Be encouraged as you continue this life journey, because that's what it is. As we place our trust in Him and reveal our willingness to stay the course, may He bless us and keep us to Himself, especially when the pathway is dark or cloudy, and we cannot see the next step.

This is just one of many books that deal with the Christian's journey, and there are many stages of spiritual growth. I pray that this book helps its readers to prosper as their souls prosper. We need to recognize the fact that there are hurting people on the battlefield that need help getting up. Some may even need to be carried off in our arms.

And I pray that you will be victorious over whatever fears you are fighting, because perfect love casts out fear. Let's strive, also, to have patience with each other, and with ourselves. We won't always get it right, but we should never stop trying. We can begin to see that when we are pressed on every side, that is often an indication that we are near the finish line.

We shouldn't be surprised when God puts people in our paths that are unlovable or hard to get along with. It is then that we need to seek God and humble ourselves because God has been known to move one and send two more in his/her place. And sometimes people who rub us the wrong way are like sandpaper…sent to rub off our rough edges.

We need to be reminded that God's thoughts are always higher than our thoughts, and that His ways are higher than ours. We can be thankful that there is always something new to learn about Him every day of our lives. And we can be set free from the traps that Satan has laid for us.

Praise God and be thankful in all things. "Do not be anxious about anything, but in every situation, by prayer and petition, with thanksgiving, present your requests to God." (Philippians 4:6, NIV)

And once our focus is on Him, He will reveal our calling, and He will do mighty works through us. All praise, glory, and honor to God the Father of the living Son of God, Jesus Christ, and the Holy Spirit.

www.ingramcontent.com/pod-product-compliance
Lightning Source LLC
Chambersburg PA
CBHW080617110526
44587CB00040BB/3734